THE ULTIMATE RIDDLE GAME FOR KIDS

THE ULTIMATE
RIDDLE GAME
FOR KIDS

A Mind-Bending Book
to Test Your Logic

Z Kids · New York

Copyright © 2022 by Penguin Random House LLC
All rights reserved.
Published in the United States by Z Kids, an imprint of Zeitgeist™,
a division of Penguin Random House LLC, New York.
penguinrandomhouse.com
Zeitgeist™ is a trademark of Penguin Random House LLC
ISBN: 9780593436028
Ebook ISBN: 9780593435748
Book design by Emma Hall
Edited by Erin Nelson and Sarah Curley
Printed in the United States of America
1 3 5 7 9 10 8 6 4 2
First Edition

CONTENTS

INTRODUCTION

Welcome to *The Ultimate Riddle Game for Kids*! In the pages ahead, get ready for tricky wordplay, mind-tickling riddles, and challenging brain teasers. You'll have to think outside the box if you want to crack these head-scratching puzzles—and stump your friends and family while you're at it!

Did you know that there are all sorts of ways of thinking? To solve these riddles, you'll have to use lateral thinking. That means you'll have to think about a problem or situation differently than how it is presented. Use your creativity and don't limit yourself to what is the most obvious answer. Sometimes you'll have to use book smarts (which you learn in school) and other times real-world smarts (which you learn on the playground) to solve the problems in this book. Experimenting with riddles is not only fun, but it also helps you solve everyday problems by training your mind to observe things others might not see.

If you can't solve a riddle, that's OK! The way to improve at something is to practice. So try another one, and practice with as many riddles as you can. The more riddles you try to solve, the better you'll get at it. And before long, you'll be a riddle expert challenging your friends and family!

Good luck! And remember, have fun!

HOW TO PLAY WITH OTHERS

It wouldn't be the Ultimate Riddle Game unless we gave you more than one way to play the game. If you think about it, your first riddle is to figure out which way you and your friends or family want to play.

You can:

1) Tally by chapter: Use separate pieces of paper to work out your riddles. When you think you have it, circle your answer. Answer as many riddles as you can throughout the chapter before you check your answers in the back of the book. (That way, you can't sneak peeks as you go.) Use the tally sheets at the end of each chapter to keep track of your score. The person who solves the most riddles correctly at the end of the chapter wins that chapter. Then the person who wins the most chapters is crowned the Ultimate Riddle Champion!

2) Tally the whole book: If you want to try riddles from different chapters, maybe hopping back and forth between chapters as you play, you'll want to go for this option. Instead of tallying at the end of each chapter, work your way through the whole book before you check your answers. (You'll want to use separate sheets of paper for this way to play, too.) Use the Ultimate Tally sheet in the back of the book to record the riddles you answered correctly. The person with the highest number of total riddles solved is the Ultimate Riddle Champion!

No matter which way you play, it works to play one-on-one with someone or with a whole bunch of people. Either way, the highest number of riddles solved wins!

HOW TO
PLAY SOLO

While this book is a game you can play with others, it is also something you can do alone. Keep track of how many riddles you solve on your own, and notice if it's easier to solve riddles the more you practice. You can also try timing yourself to see if your riddle-solving gets any faster as you go!

1

?

TRICKY QUICK-HITTERS

QUICK-HITTER RIDDLES ARE SHORT, tricky questions. The entire riddle can be one question or a couple of sentences followed by a short question. They usually have wordplay—words that sound alike or have more than one meaning—which you'll need to use lateral thinking to figure out. When you're trying to solve a quick-hitter riddle, read the riddle more than once. Sometimes we miss information the first time we read something. These types of riddles often use double meanings to confuse us, so pay extra attention to words that can mean more than one thing. Last but not least, don't think too hard. Oftentimes, the answer is more obvious than it first appears!

1

What is the capital of California?

2

I'm all ears, but I won't hear anything you say. What am I?

3

Aisha places something on the table. She cuts it, but she would never eat it. What does Aisha put on the table?

4

I may have an eye, but don't ask me to look at anything. What am I?

5

What has five eyes and is between two pieces of land?

6

What falls but doesn't injure itself?

7

This object circles the globe from a corner. What is it?

8

Celine, Phoebe, and Brenden are drinking coffee. Louis, Harper, and Elijah are drinking tea. What will Esme drink?

9

I live in a house with no doors or windows, but I have no privacy. I can't leave on my own, and my food comes from the sky. What am I?

10

The green part is ripe. The red part is edible. The black part is spat out. What is it?

11

A taxi driver was on a busy street in the city. She texted, turned the wrong way down a one-way street, and crossed at two red lights without stopping. Several police officers saw her do all these things, but they never gave her a ticket. How come?

12

Every night, Rickelle, Kenna, Tahra, and Jean sit down to play together. They play for money, but no one loses. How come?

13

Selva says that at the top of this there is a bottom. What is it?

14

Dylan was driving a black SUV without the lights on. The moon was not out. A person was in the middle of the road. He did not hit them. How did Dylan see them?

15

Zahara's uncle has six nieces: Adina, Dorit, Aimee, Danah, Asha; what's the sixth one's name?

16

An SUV, a minivan, a convertible, and a sedan arrive at a four-way stop. They can't decide who should go first, so they all start moving at the same time. All four vehicles pass through the intersection, and there are no accidents. How?

17

All day, while Carlos ran errands, it snowed. Carlos wasn't wearing a head covering nor did he carry an umbrella, yet the only hair that got wet was in his beard. Why?

18

During free time in their classroom, Naisaiah read a graphic novel, Nicholl painted with watercolors, Darnel played chess, and Tristen played a computer game. What did Chasity do?

19

My dwelling is just big enough for me. If I want to leave it, I have to destroy it. Once I'm out, there's no going back. What am I?

20

Ansel says he knows something that gets soggy as it dries. What is he talking about?

21

For work, Mateo stares at faces then fixes them. What is Mateo's job?

22

Why can't someone living in Washington State be buried in Vancouver, Canada?

23

Byram is camping with his family. They have one match to light a campfire, a mosquito-repellent candle, and a lantern. Which should Byram light first?

24

On the first day of a comics convention, Asia asked 100 people the same question. Each person gave a different answer, but they were all correct. What was the question Asia asked?

25

Sangeeta lives in a one-story apartment. She loves the color turquoise, so she decorated the inside of her apartment in shades of turquoise. The carpet is turquoise, the walls are turquoise, the furniture is turquoise. Even her refrigerator is turquoise! So what color are the stairs inside her apartment?

26

Hakeem says he can prove there are less than 20 seconds in a year. How?

27

Can you drop a full mug without spilling any coffee?

28

A baboon, a buzzard, and a gecko are trying to get to the top of a palm tree. Who will be the first one to reach the banana?

29

Miriam walked into her house and found Julie and Laura struggling to breathe. There was water and shards of glass everywhere. What happened?

30

Gemma says that to use something you have to break it first. What is she talking about?

31

Mackenzie is a window washer. On Monday, her client had a 20-story apartment complex. She fell while washing one of the apartment's windows but did not get hurt. Why not?

32

Isaac was in the back seat of his mom's station wagon when he saw four doors appear out of nowhere: one was platinum, one was wooden, one was pearl, and one was brick. Out of all the doors, which did he go through first?

33

People look right through me, but I can make a pail feel less heavy. What am I?

34

A carrot, a top hat, and two buttons are on the lawn in front of Clark's house. If no one placed these items on Clark's lawn, how did they get there?

35

How many letters are in the alphabet?

36

In Dupree, South Dakota, someone can't take a photo of a person with sunglasses. Why not?

37

Lourdes stands behind Silas while Silas stands behind Lourdes. How is this possible?

38

Elsie draws a square. Without touching it, how can Elsie make the square bigger?

39

Ms. Jacobsen's children are playing in a field on the other side of a pond. Ms. Jacobsen shouts to the children that it's time for dinner. The children cross the pond without getting wet and don't use a bridge or a boat. How?

40

Mx. Thoreau is thinking of a four-letter word. They write the word forward. Then they write it backward. Then they write it upside down. Any which way, Mx. Thoreau can still read the word. What word are they thinking of?

41

Anastasia is thinking of an object. The object has a frame, but there aren't any pictures in it. The object has arms but no hands. What is it?

42

You're driving a shuttle bus for the airport. At the airport parking lot, 10 people get on. At the first terminal, four people get off. At the second terminal, three more people get off, and at the third terminal, the rest of the passengers get off. What color are the shuttle driver's eyes?

43

What part of New Jersey is in New York?

44

Most people can barely hold me, even though I don't weigh anything at all. What am I?

45

Two words on their own have just a few letters, but put them together and they hold the most. What are they?

46

Fill in the next letter: JFMAMJJASON___.

47

Jeanette is thinking of a five-letter word. If Jeanette drops the first letter, it will make you sick. What word is Jeanette thinking of?

48

What is the center of gravity?

49

Food increases me while water decreases me.
What am I?

50

I can be both good and bad inside your body.
What am I?

51

What can Saul grip with his right hand but not with
his left?

52

I sit and wait for my victims to be gathered. Then with a single sharp jab I pierce them with my pointy teeth and make them one. What am I?

53

Jessamyn is still hungry after dinner. They look inside the refrigerator and open a jar of pickles, a juice box, and a leftovers container. What was the first thing they opened?

54

Sometimes I am hard, while other times I'm not. I run hot and cold. I can rush, but I can also be still. What am I?

55

One of these words is different: *stun, ton, evil, letter, mood, bad, snap, straw.* Which one is it?

56

Sylvana says this can't move, even though it has two legs. What is it?

57

What's constantly moving but doesn't use its bed to rest?

58

You have something but don't use it nearly as much as other people do. What is it?

59

I may have three feet, but they are no help with standing, walking, or running. What am I?

60

At its beginning, this object is long. But by the end, it's short. What is it?

61

The more this object is used, the brighter it gets. What is it?

62

Janssen says this can fill a stadium without taking up any space. What is it?

63

In front of you I always lie, though invisible to the naked eye. What am I?

64

My hands can't hold anything and my face has no expression. What am I?

65

Even though I get cut up and sliced, my attacker is the one who cries. What am I?

66

I'm around the same age as the planet, but every month I'm reborn. What am I?

67

What could run around a building without going anywhere?

68

One can keep me, two can share me, but three make me nonexistent. What am I?

69

Everyone is always doing the same thing at the same time. What is it?

70

I can hear this, but I can't see it. I can speak to it, but it will never speak first. What is it?

71

There is one thing that everyone agrees smells better than it tastes. What is it?

72

It goes through a locked gate but doesn't enter or leave. What is it?

73

What originates with T, concludes with T, and contains T?

74

Catia brought something to the picnic, but no one ate it. What did she bring?

75

Miley says you can catch something, but you can't throw it. What is she talking about?

76

What is substantial when forward but not when reversed?

77

All the following words have something in common: *revive, banana, grammar, voodoo, assess, potato, dresser, uneven*. What is it?

78

Reagan says that she can spell the word *enemy* with only three letters. How?

79

How are the letter *a* and 12:00 p.m. similar?

80

What can we sometimes see when it's made, but never after it's made?

81

What comes after the last *F* in this sequence? ETTFF__

82

Less of it is visible the more it appears. What is it?

83

Its neck doesn't hold up a head, and its arms lack hands. What is it?

84

Where does fifteen come before fourteen?

85

Petunia picked up a pile of papers off the porch. Can you spell that without any *P*s?

86

This is the same size as a giraffe and weightless. What is it?

87

Jasmine is thinking of a five-letter word. It is something eaten in almost every country in the world. If Jasmine drops the first letter in the word, the new word is something you need to boil water. If she drops the first two letters, the new word is something you do to food. If she mixes up the last three letters, the new word is a tasty beverage. What word is Jasmine thinking of?

TALLY YOUR POINTS

CHAPTER 1: TRICKY QUICK-HITTERS

Make sure you've read through "How to Play with Others" (page 8). Use this tally sheet if you are playing winners by chapter. Write the players' names in the left column and use the right column to tally your correct answers. You can use hash marks or write down the riddle numbers you answered correctly. (Tip: Tracking the riddle numbers will help you remember which riddles you've already mastered!)

PLAYER	SCORE

PLAYER

SCORE

MATH MONSTERS

THE RIDDLES IN THIS section all have something to do with numbers. For some riddles, you'll have to do actual calculations or use logic, but for others, you'll simply think about how numbers can relate to each other. Read each riddle carefully and think about what it is asking. Try strategies like visualizing or using pen and paper to work out the problem. Finally, don't get discouraged—making mistakes is part of the process!

88

Five friends are sitting at a table having a snack. On the table there is a plate with five cookies. Each friend takes one cookie. There is one cookie left on the plate. How is this possible?

89

Seven is even in just one step. What is it?

90

Five plus eight equals 13, but it can also equal one. How?

91

Nikita's neighborhood is having a tag sale. Nikita is selling one type of item. When they sell five the price is $0.25; when they sell 82 the price is $0.50. But when they sell 121 the price is only $0.75 cents. What is Nikita selling?

92

In a half marathon, Raquel finished three places in front of the last person and one ahead of Lisa, who came in fourth. How many runners were there?

93

Ahmed has been timing how fast he can clean his room. Every day, he gets a little faster. Today, he wants to try to clean his room in 15 minutes, but he only has 11- and 7-minute sand timers. How can he use the sand timers to track exactly 15 minutes?

94

At a party, a grandma mingled while eating an appetizer. Two moms each ate an appetizer while chatting with their friends. Two daughters caught up with pals while each eating an appetizer. How many appetizers were eaten in total?

95

An electric train is leaving from Boston and traveling south to Baltimore. It is moving at a speed of 55 miles per hour. There is a strong wind coming from the west. In what direction will the smoke from the locomotive blow?

96

Compare a pound of metal to a pound of Bubble Wrap. Which weighs more?

97

During a baseball game, Lyssa was the first up to bat for her team of nine players. There were no substitutions or changes in her team's batting order during the game, which lasted nine innings. What is the least number of runs Lyssa's team could have scored?

98

What is 3/5 chili, 2/7 cabbage, and 2/5 gouda?

99

When Grace was traveling to Los Angeles, she met a person who had 10 siblings. The 10 siblings had 20 children, the 20 children had 30 pets, and the 30 pets had 50 toys. How many siblings, children, pets, and toys were going to Los Angeles?

100

Lucinia is thinking of three numbers. Abed asks what the sum of the three numbers is. Then he asks what the product of the three numbers is. Abed is surprised to hear that they are the same number. How can that be?

101

Next year, Claudia is turning 11 years old. The day before yesterday, Claudia was 8. On what day was Claudia born?

102

Siân owes Jordano $15. She gives him two bills. One of the bills is not a $5 bill. What bills does Siân give Jordano?

103

A few years ago, Cecilia was 12 years old. Cecilia's cousin was half as old as her. Now, Cecilia is 18. How old is Cecilia's cousin?

104

There are two kangaroos in front of a kangaroo, two kangaroos behind a kangaroo, and one kangaroo in the middle. How many kangaroos are there in total?

105

Lee wants to take her friends to a concert—she's even going to pay for their tickets! Is it cheaper for Lee to take one friend to two concerts or two friends to one concert?

106

The Martinez family are hiking and they come across an underground tunnel. Dad can walk through the tunnel in one minute. Papa can walk through in two minutes. Robin can do it in four minutes and Suzanna can walk through in five minutes. Only two family members can go through the tunnel at a time, and they can't move any faster than the slowest moving person in the pair. Can the Martinezes make it to the other side if they have a flashlight that lasts only 12 minutes and they are afraid of the dark?

107

Karry is managing a construction crew of 10 workers. Her team is fixing a roof. It takes them one week to finish the job. How long would it take five people to fix the same roof?

108

Estevan has a cookie business, and he needs to fulfill orders for some of his bigger customers. One shipping crate can hold 10 medium-size boxes or 8 jumbo-size boxes. Estevan mailed 96 boxes in one shipment. The number of medium-size boxes was less than the number of jumbo-size boxes. How many crates did Estevan mail in one shipment?

109

At the school supply store, a pencil is 40 cents, an eraser is 60 cents, and a notebook is 80 cents. How much is a pen?

110

In Mr. Jacoby's fifth-grade class, there are 15 students. Eight of his students are wearing jackets and 10 are wearing scarves. Five kids are wearing both. How many aren't wearing outerwear?

111

Rowan pays $7 for a crow, $28 for a tarantula, and $21 for a bee. How much money would Rowan pay for a horse?

112

What is the next number in the series? 8,213; 3,821; 1,382; ___

113

Clarence is grocery shopping and purchases a dozen eggs. On his way home, all but five break. How many eggs are left?

114

Sanjay argues that with one straight line he can make the following equation true: 7 + 2 + 8 = 750. How is that possible?

115

Charlotte and Magdalena are on a train leaving Seattle. Charlotte lets Magdalena have the window seat so she can look at the scenery. After a few minutes, Magdalena says, "I've noticed that the trains going in the other direction pass us every five minutes. How many trains do you think arrive in Seattle every hour if trains are going the same speed in both directions?" Charlotte answers, "Well, that's easy! Twelve—because 60 divided by 5 equals 12." Is Charlotte correct?

116

Pilar is going rock climbing with their best friends in a couple of weeks, so they're practicing in a rock-climbing gym. One of the walls is 10 feet tall. In one hour, Pilar climbs five feet, then falls four feet. If Pilar continues doing this, how many hours will it take them to reach the top of the climbing wall?

117

Diego is having a family dinner with his siblings. He has the same number of brothers as he does sisters, but each of Diego's sisters has twice the number of brothers as she does sisters. How many place settings does Diego need to set the table for?

118

Jim tells Mike he was born in 1982. But Mike remembers going to Jim's 11th birthday party two Saturdays ago. Jim isn't lying. How is this possible?

119

There is something unique about the number 854,917,632. What is it?

120

Cristiano is 20 meters away from his treehouse. Every time he makes a move toward the treehouse, he covers half the distance. In how many moves will Cristiano reach the treehouse?

121

Before the rugby match, Jhumpa tells Oliver that she knows the score will be 0–0. How did she know this?

122

How many wooden planks does it take to complete a five-mile-long boardwalk on a beach?

123

There are several coffee mugs on a kitchen shelf. If one mug is the fifth from the right and seventh from the left, how many mugs are on the shelf?

124

What answer will Gino get if he divides 210 by half and subtracts 10?

125

Ms. Rudolph writes the following question on the whiteboard: *What is half of eight plus eight?* "I know!" says Ginny. "It's eight." Ms. Rudolph replies, "I'm sorry, Ginny, but that's not the right answer." What is the right answer?

126

Leon says he can go from 704 to 280 with just one letter. How?

127

Sayantani is the lead vet tech for a farm animal rescue organization. She just finished giving some newly arrived pigs their medical check-ups, and now they're ready to be fed. When she tries to put each pig in its own pen, she ends up with one pig too many. But if she puts two pigs in each pen, then she has one pen too many. How many pigs and pens does Sayantani have?

128

What can you put between zero and one to make the result greater than zero, but less than one?

129

A farmer in Iowa owns an apple tree. She sells fruit at a local farmers' market. A customer who usually comes every week is going out of town and wants to put in an order so his kitchen will be fully stocked upon his return. He asks the farmer what's the most fruit he can purchase. The farmer knows that the tree has 20 branches. Each branch has eight boughs, and each bough has four twigs. Since each twig bears one piece of fruit, how many apricots will the farmer be able to sell?

130

There are three sons in the Davis family. Each of these sons has a sister. How many children are in the Davis family?

131

There are 24 slices of cheese in a pack. You take away two. How many slices of cheese do you have now?

132

Camryn works in a bakery and is making a cake. They need exactly four cups of flour. All the measuring cups are dirty, so Camryn has to use two different containers to measure flour. One container can hold five cups and the other can hold three cups. How can Camryn measure exactly four cups of flour using the two containers?

133

Rhian and Fiona are playing with toy cars. Fiona said, "It isn't fair that you have three times as many cars as I do!" Rhian replied, "Ugh, fine!" and gave Fiona 10 more toy cars. Fiona argued, "You still have twice as many as I do!" How many more cars must Rhian give Fiona for them to have the same number?

TALLY YOUR POINTS

CHAPTER 2: MATH MONSTERS

Make sure you've read through "How to Play with Others" (page 8). Use this tally sheet if you are playing winners by chapter. Write the players' names in the left column and use the right column to tally your correct answers. You can use hash marks or write down the riddle numbers you answered correctly. (Tip: Tracking the riddle numbers will help you remember which riddles you've already mastered!)

PLAYER   SCORE

PLAYER   **SCORE**

3

SNEAKY
STORIES

NOW THAT YOU'VE CONQUERED the riddles in chapters 1 and 2, take the skills you've learned and try to solve these longer storylike riddles. The riddles in this final chapter are a bit trickier, so you'll need to take time to think through each problem. These in-depth riddles will definitely give your brain a workout, so try breaking them down into chunks. Remember, riddles are meant to trick you. Keep an eye out for language that could have double meanings, and don't assume anything. Good luck!

134

After school, Gerard tells his brother Matthew that he found a $10 bill. Matthew says, "Hey, that's mine! I left it on the counter." "No, it's not," says Gerard. "I found it between pages 115 and 116 of the book I'm reading." "You're lying and I can prove it," Matthew says smugly. How does Matthew know Gerard is lying?

135

There is a lamp inside Tasslyn's basement. The door to the basement is closed, and she cannot see if the lamp is on or off through the door. However, she knows the lamp is off to start with. In the hallway leading to the basement door, there is a panel with three switches, but only one switch controls the lamp in the basement. Tasslyn can flip the switches however many times she wants, but once she opens the door, she can no longer touch the switches. How does she figure out which switch controls the lamp?

136

While on a conservation expedition in the Amazon rainforest, Professor Tatiana felt something in the pocket of her cargo pants. She knew it didn't have legs, but it had a head and a tail. When the professor walked around, she could feel it moving inside her pocket. However, Professor Tatiana wasn't worried or scared and went about her work. Why wasn't the professor concerned?

137

Last year while vacationing at a big lake, Rahul went on a group fishing expedition. The group stopped off at a small island for a picnic lunch. Rahul decided he would rather take a nap, so he found some shade and fell asleep. When he woke up, everyone was gone—including the fishing boat that dropped him off! He'd left his phone on the boat and didn't know how to swim, so he waited for someone to save him, but no one came. Rahul was stranded! A few months later, though, he got off the island. How did he do it?

138

Karuna is at the school fair with her friends. Mr. Ines is guessing students' heights. Mr. Ines says, "Karuna, if I write your exact height on this piece of paper, you owe me $20, but if I can't, I will pay you $20." Karuna agrees, thinking she can outsmart Mr. Ines and lie about her height. Mr. Ines looks at Karuna, then writes something on a piece of paper. He folds it up and hands it to her, a satisfied smirk on his face. Karuna opens the piece of paper and her mouth drops open in shock. She reaches into her wallet and hands off a crisp $20 bill. How did Mr. Ines win the bet?

139

LeVar is stuck in a building with only two ways out. If he uses the front exit, he will encounter a giant magnifying glass through which the fiery hot sun will burn him. If he goes out the back exit, he will meet a fire-breathing dragon. Which exit does LeVar use to escape?

140

After a group of high school hockey players finish practice, some of them decide to take the bus home. They're all carrying their brand-new hockey sticks, which are each a little over five feet long. The bus driver stops them before they get on and tells them they can't bring anything longer than five feet on the bus. The players go back inside the hockey rink, get something, and come back out. Now, the bus driver lets them on the bus. What did they get from the hockey rink, and what did they do with it?

141

The Newton family is on vacation, and they are staying in the penthouse suite of a 10-story hotel. Every day, Jamie and his siblings take the elevator down to the lobby and go to the pool. When they come back for lunch, they take the elevator to the fifth floor and then walk up five flights of stairs to get back to their room. Why?

142

The Phams live in a big round house. The Phams love to travel and collect trinkets from every place they go. They display their souvenirs all over the house so that no matter what room you're in, you'll have something interesting to look at it. One night, when Mr. and Mrs. Pham return from a long day at work, they notice that one of their favorite souvenirs displayed in the living room is broken. They ask their children if any of them accidentally broke the souvenir while they were doing their chores. Justina says she was making her bed, Carolina says she was dusting the corners of her room, and Maxie says she was putting away the dishes in the kitchen. Who's lying and actually broke the souvenir?

143

A grandmother wanted to gift a special family heirloom to one of her three grandchildren. She couldn't decide which one to give it to, so she decided to have a little competition. She had them over for lemonade and cookies one afternoon and said, "I want you to buy something that is small enough to fit in my hand but big enough that it will fill my office. Whoever can complete this task will get the heirloom." They whipped out their phones and immediately started searching for something to buy Grandma. A few days later, they all met up again. Grandma asked each grandchild to come into her office and try to fill it up with their item. Molly came in and showed her grandma the pieces of felt she bought. She laid them across the room, but they barely covered the floor. Mac came in and pulled out the slime he bought, but he couldn't stretch it far enough to cover the floor either. Finally, Laurel came in and showed her grandmother what she bought. Grandma was pleasantly surprised and announced to Molly and Mac that Laurel had won the contest. What did Laurel show her grandmother?

144

There is a box full of hats. Three are purple and two are green. Saladin, Amari, and Keisa line up behind one another, close their eyes, and pick a hat to wear. Saladin is behind Amari and Keisa, so he can see the others' hats; Amari is in the middle, so he can only see Keisa's hat; and Keisa is in the front and can't see anyone's hat. Saladin says he doesn't know what color hat he's wearing. Then Amari says the same thing. But Keisa knows exactly what color hat she's wearing. What color is Keisa's hat?

145

Sawako says to Luiza, "Did you know I know a song for every name that's ever existed?" Luiza laughs and says, "Prove it!" Sawako then says, "Give me a name, any name, and I'll sing you a song with that name in it." Luiza laughs again and says, "OK, how about my dog's name, Mr. Fudd?" Minutes later, Sawako finishes the song and has a big old grin on her face. Luiza says, "Wow, I guess you were right!" What song did Sawako sing?

A fairy queen had a birdcage with beautiful golden finches in her throne room. The finches were given to her by her father right before he went off to war. She never saw her father again, so those finches became her most prized possessions. One day, one of the finches went missing. She gathered all her subjects and told them that if no one confessed to taking the bird, she would make them all pass a test. No one said a word. She had her royal guard line everyone up. One by one, they had to enter a dark room. In that dark room was a filthy box covered in charcoal dust. Inside the box sat a magical rooster. Each person had to touch the box. When the thief touched the box, the rooster would crow, and the queen would know who took her finch. Everyone went into the room, but the rooster never crowed. "Your Majesty, it couldn't have been any of us; the rooster didn't crow!" said one of her subjects. "Oh, but it was one of you. And I know which one," the queen said with a twinkle in her eye. How did the queen know who the thief was?

147

There are three bins: one is labeled "Crayons," one is labeled "Markers," and one is labeled "Crayons and Markers." The bins weren't labeled correctly, so none of the labels identifies what is actually in each bin. Cassandra opens one of the bins. Without looking in the bin, she takes out one item. If she just looks at the item, how can Cassandra immediately label all the bins correctly?

148

Kwame finds a treasure chest guarded by a troll who offers him a red key, a blue key, and a gold key. Only one of them can open the treasure chest, and he has only one chance to choose the right key. Behind the troll, Kwame sees a cipher that reads, "TON HLK EDE GEY." He instantly knows what key to choose. Which one does he choose?

149

Mr. Ohi is traveling with a snake, a mouse, and a bag of grains when he arrives at a river. Mr. Ohi has a boat, but it can only carry him and one other thing. If the snake and the mouse are left together on the riverbank, the snake will eat the mouse. If the mouse and the grains are left together, the mouse will eat the grains. How does Mr. Ohi get everything across?

150

Two after-school clubs meet at the same time. One of the clubs is so secretive that the members lie about anything having to do with the club to nonmembers. The other club is very open and welcoming, and the members will answer any questions about the club truthfully. Ramona, who helps out in the office, has to get a message to one of the members in the club of truth-tellers, but she doesn't know which classroom they meet in. A member from one of the clubs is standing in the hallway outside the two classrooms where the clubs meet. Ramona approaches the member and asks him one question. From the club member's answer, she knows which classroom to go to. What did Ramona ask?

151

Rabia is at the library and needs to use one of the computers to do some research. She's used the computer so often that she's memorized the password. Except this time, she can't log in. She tries twice, but the password doesn't work. Suddenly Rabia remembers that the librarians reset the passwords every two months for security purposes. So Rabia goes to the circulation desk and says, "Excuse me, the password on the second computer is expired." The librarian replies, "Yes, that's right. The password is changed. Listen carefully. I am sure you can figure out the new one. The new one has the same number of letters as the old password, but only two of the letters are the same." "Oh, I see!" said Rabia. With that, Rabia could correctly log in to the research computer. What are both the new and old passwords?

152

Brionn is driving across state and stops to rest in West Hickory. He notices something strange about the town. In the bookstore, there are books, but no pages. In people's yards, there are trees, but no branches. At the local diner, there are eggs, but no bacon. And all the buildings have doors, yet no entrances or exits. What is special about West Hickory?

153

Izzy loves playing video games, but her stepdad doesn't love how much time she spends playing them. He tried everything to get her to stop and hang out with the rest of the family, including ice cream for dinner and trips to the comic book store, but Izzy would always go back to her video games. One day, Izzy's stepdad was so fed up that he came up with a more permanent solution. He went into the garage, got his toolbox, and fixed the problem. Now Izzy couldn't use her video game console anymore, but her stepdad could if he wanted to. What did Izzy's stepdad do?

154

Five people live on the same floor of an apartment building, and their apartments are numbered #1 through #5. Each apartment door is made from a different material. Each resident has a job, a favorite drink, a car, and a pet. But none of the residents have the same job, favorite drink, car, or pet. Here are some clues:

- The teacher lives in the apartment with the brick door.

- The author has a pet dog.

- The graphic designer drinks tea.

- The apartment with the metal door is to the left of the one with the wood door.

- The resident who lives in the apartment with the metal door drinks coffee.

- The resident who drives an SUV has birds.

- The resident who lives in the apartment with the cement door drives a convertible.

- The resident living in apartment #3 drinks milk.

- The nurse lives in apartment #1.

- The resident who drives a sedan lives next to the one who has a cat.

- The resident who has an iguana lives next to the one who drives a convertible.

- The resident who drives a van drinks orange juice.

- The local business owner rides a motorcycle.

- The nurse lives next to the apartment with the glass door.

- The resident who drives a sedan lives next to the one who drinks water.

So what is the job of the resident who has a fish?

TALLY YOUR POINTS

CHAPTER 3: SNEAKY STORIES

Make sure you've read through "How to Play with Others" (page 8). Use this tally sheet if you are playing winners by chapter. Write the players' names in the left column and use the right column to tally your correct answers. You can use hash marks or write down the riddle numbers you answered correctly. (Tip: Tracking the riddle numbers will help you remember which riddles you've already mastered!)

PLAYER	SCORE

PLAYER

SCORE

ANSWERS

CHAPTER 1: TRICKY QUICK-HITTERS

1.   The letter *C* is the only capital in California.

2.   a field of corn

3.   a deck of cards

4.   a needle

5.   the Mississippi River

6.   snow, rain, or water

7.   a stamp

8.   Coffee, because Esme has two *E*s, just like all the coffee drinkers.

9.   a fish in a fishbowl or aquarium

10. a watermelon

11. She was walking, not driving.

12. They are in a band, and they are playing a concert where they all get paid.

13. your legs

14. It was a bright, sunny day.

15. Zahara

16. They all turned right.

17. Carlos is bald.

18. Chasity played chess with Darnel.

19. a chick in an egg

20. a towel

21. He is a watchmaker.

22. They can't be buried because they are still alive.

23. the match

24. What time is it?

25. Sangeeta lives in a one-story apartment, so there are no stairs.

26. There are 12 seconds in a year: January second, February second, March second, April second, May second, and so on.

27. Yes, when it is filled with hot chocolate.

28. None of them, because bananas don't grow on palm trees.

29. Julie and Laura are fish and their bowl was knocked over.

30. an egg

31. Mackenzie was washing a first-floor apartment window, so she was still on the ground.

32. the car door

33. a hole

34. They were used by someone who made a snowperson. The snow has now melted.

35. There are 11 letters in "the alphabet."

36. You can't use sunglasses to take a photo. You need a camera to take a photo.

37. They stand back-to-back.

38. Elsie can draw a smaller square next to it. Now the first square is bigger.

39. The pond is frozen.

40. NOON

41. a pair of eyeglasses

42. You are the shuttle driver, so the answer is whatever color eyes you have.

43. New

44. breath

45. post office

46. The letter *D*. The pattern contains the first letter of each month.

47. music

48. the letter *v*

49. fire

50. bacteria

51. his left elbow

52. a stapler

53. the refrigerator door

54. water

55. The word *letter* is different. If you read each word backward, *letter* is the only one that doesn't make another word.

56. a pair of pants

57. a river

58. your name

59. a yardstick

60. a candle

61. a brain

62. noise

63. the future

64. a clock

65. an onion

66. the moon

67. a fence

68. a secret

69. growing older

70. an echo

71. a nose

72. a keyhole

73. a teapot

74. Cutlery, a blanket, a basket, or anything else you would use but wouldn't eat at a picnic.

75. a cold

76. the word *ton*

77. Take the first letter of each word and place it at the end. It will spell the same word backward.

78. F-O-E

79. They're both the middle of day.

80. a sound

81. The letter *S*. Each letter is the first letter in the numbers eleven, twelve, thirteen, fourteen, fifteen.

82. darkness

83. a shirt

84. in the dictionary

85. T-H-A-T

86. a giraffe's shadow

87. wheat

CHAPTER 2: MATH MONSTERS

88. The person to take the last cookie also took the plate.

89. Take away the *s*.

90. When you're looking at a clock. If you start at the number five on a clockface and count eight spots, you'll land on the number one.

91. Nikita is selling address numbers, and they each cost $0.25.

92. There were six runners. Raquel came in third place.

93. Ahmed should flip both timers over at the same time, but not start cleaning yet. When the seven-minute timer is up, there are still four minutes left on the other timer. Now he should start cleaning. When the four minutes are up, he can flip the 11-minute timer over and let it run out: 4 + 11 = 15 minutes total.

94. Three. The grandma is also a mom, and the mom is also a daughter.

95. Electric trains don't produce smoke.

96. Neither. They each weigh one pound. A pound is a pound no matter the object.

97. Zero. In the first inning, Lyssa and the next two batters walk, so bases are loaded. Then the next three strike out, ending the team's time up to bat. In the second inning, the first three players walk, so the bases are loaded again, and Lyssa is back to bat. She strikes out, and so do the next two batters. In the third inning, the first three players walk and the next three strike out. Lyssa is back at the plate at the start of the fourth inning. This pattern is now repeated until the game ends with zero runs.

98. Chicago

99. Zero. Grace was the only one going to Los Angeles.

100. Lucinia is thinking of the numbers one, two, and three. When added together, the sum is six. When multiplied, the product is also six.

101. December 31; today is January 1.

102. A $10 bill and a $5 bill. One of the bills isn't a $5 bill, but the other one is.

103. Her cousin is 12. Half of 12 is six, so Cecilia's cousin is six years younger than her. When Cecilia is 18, her cousin is still six years younger and is now 12.

104. three

105. It's cheaper to take two friends to one concert because Lee only has to buy three tickets. If she took one friend to two concerts, she'd have to buy four tickets in all.

106. Yes. First, Dad and Papa go, and it takes them two minutes. Then, Dad comes back with the flashlight in one minute. Next, Robin and Suzanna go through in five minutes and hand off the flashlight to Papa. Papa brings the flashlight back to Dad in two minutes. Then, it takes them two minutes to go back through and meet up with their children. Therefore: 2 + 1 + 5 + 2 + 2 = 12.

107. It will take them no time to fix the roof—because the roof is already fixed!

108. The answer is 11 crates. If Estevan mailed a total of 96 boxes, then the jumbo-size boxes in the crates must be a multiple of 8, which means he used either 16 or 56 jumbo-size boxes. Since there are more jumbo-size boxes in the crates then medium-size ones, the number of jumbo-size boxes must be 56. There are 96 – 56 = 40 medium-size boxes. Then divide the total number of each type of box by how many boxes can fit into a crate to figure out how many crates Estevan used in total: (56 ÷ 8) + (40 ÷ 10) = 7 + 4 = 11.

109. 20 cents. To calculate the price of each school supply, multiply the number of vowels in the word by 20 cents.

110. Two students aren't wearing outerwear. We know that five students are wearing both a scarf and a jacket. That means three students are wearing only jackets [8 – 5 = 3] and five students are wearing only scarves [10 – 5 = 5]. That's eight students total who are wearing either a jacket or a scarf. 8 + 5 = 13 students are wearing some combination of outerwear, so 15 students – 13 students = 2 students are not wearing outerwear.

111. Rowan would pay $14, or $3.50 per leg.

112. 2,138. The last number is moved to the front to make the next number in the series.

113. five eggs

114. Draw a line on the first plus sign to turn it into a four. The equation then becomes true: 742 + 8 = 750.

115. If Charlotte and Magdalena were on a train that wasn't moving, then Charlotte's calculations would have been correct, but their train *was* moving. After meeting the first train, it took five minutes to meet a second train, but it took the second train five more minutes to reach where Magdalena and Charlotte met the first train. So, the time between trains is 10 minutes, not five, and only six trains arrive in Seattle every hour.

116. It will take Pilar six hours. In the first hour, Pilar reaches a height of five feet, then falls four feet; thus, ending at the height of one foot. In the second hour, they reach six feet but fall to two feet. In the third hour, Pilar reaches seven feet but falls back to three feet. In the fourth hour, Pilar reaches eight feet but falls back to four feet. In the fifth hour, they reach nine feet but fall back to five feet. In the sixth hour, Pilar reaches 10 feet, so now they are at the top of the wall.

117. Diego should set seven place settings. There will be three brothers, three sisters, and Diego.

118. Jim was born in hospital room 1982.

119. It's the numbers one through nine in alphabetical order.

120. Cristiano will never reach the treehouse because each move is always only half the distance, no matter how small.

121. The score is always 0–0 before the game.

122. only one—the final plank

123. 11 mugs

124. The answer is 410. 210 ÷ 1/2 = 210 × 2 = 420 – 10 = 410

125. The answer is 12. One half of eight is four. [4 + 8 = 12]

126. He adds an x between 70 and four: 70 × 4 = 280.

127. Sayantani has four pigs and three pens.

128. A decimal point. Your result would be 0.1, which is between zero and one.

129. None. An apple tree cannot produce apricots.

130. There are four children. Each son has the same sister. There are three sons and one daughter.

131. You have two slices of cheese. You took away two slices and left 22 in the pack.

132. Camryn fills the five-cup container, then uses the flour in the five-cup container to fill the three-cup container. They empty the three-cup container, then pour the two remaining cups of flour from the five-cup container into the three-cup container. Camryn measures five cups of flour with the five-cup container again and uses it to fill the three-cup container to fill it. There are now exactly four cups of flour left in the five-cup container. (Alternatively, Camryn fills the five-cup container, then uses the flour in the five-cup container to fill the three-cup container. That leaves two cups in the five-cup container. They add the two cups to the cake mix and repeat the process.)

133. Rhian must give Fiona another 20 toy cars, giving them each 60. Fiona started with 30 toy cars and Rhian with 90.

CHAPTER 3: SNEAKY STORIES

134. Pages 115 and 116 are the front and back of a single page, so Gerard couldn't have found anything between them.

135. Tasslyn flips the first switch and waits a few minutes. She flips the first switch back to its original position, and then immediately flips the second switch. She opens the door. If the lamp is on, then the second switch controls it. If the lamp is off, then she feels the bulb with her hand. If the bulb is hot, the first switch controls it, and if the bulb is cold, then the third switch, the one she did not touch, controls it.

136. Professor Tatiana knew it was only a coin.

137. Rahul waited until winter when the lake froze and walked off the island to shore.

138. Mr. Ines did exactly what he said he would and wrote "your exact height" on the paper.

139. He waits until nighttime, then goes through the front exit.

140. The players got the boxes the hockey sticks came in, which are five feet long. They put their sticks in diagonally, so the entire package is now only five feet.

141. They walk the last five flights because Jamie and his siblings can't reach the buttons higher than five.

142. Carolina is fibbing. She said she was dusting the corners, but the Phams live in a round house, so there are no corners.

143. Something that brightens the room, such as a lantern or candle.

144. Keisa's hat is purple. If Amari and Keisa were both wearing green hats, then Saladin would have known that his hat was purple. Amari can only see Keisa's hat, and based on the fact that Saladin doesn't know his hat color, Amari and Keisa are either both wearing purple hats or one green and one purple. If Keisa were wearing a green hat, then Amari would know he was wearing a purple hat. But if Keisa is wearing a purple hat, Amari could be wearing either a green or a purple hat.

145. Sawako sang "Happy Birthday."

146. By touching the box, the subjects would end up with coal on their hands. The thief would have been too scared to touch the box in case the rooster crowed, so they wouldn't have any coal on their hands.

147. Cassandra first opens the bin that is labeled "Crayons and Markers." She knows that since none of the labels are correct, the bin must either contain only crayons or only markers. Suppose that she removes a crayon from that bin. Therefore, that bin must be the "Crayons Only" bin. One of the two remaining bins must be the "Markers Only" bin. However, one is labeled "Crayons Only," and the other is labeled "Markers Only." Therefore, the one labeled "Crayons Only" is the bin that contains only markers, and the bin labeled "Markers Only" is the bin that contains both crayons and markers.

148. He chooses the gold key. When you rearrange the letters in the cipher, it says "THE GOLDEN KEY."

149. Mr. Ohi carries the mouse to the other side, then returns alone. They take the snake to the other side and return with the mouse. Mr. Ohi leaves the mouse and carries the grains to the other side. They leave the grains with the snake and return alone. Finally, Mr. Ohi gets the mouse and takes it to the other side.

150. Ramona asked, "Which classroom does your club meet in?" She would then go to the classroom the member pointed to because a truthful person would point toward the correct classroom, and the liar would also point to the correct classroom since he is a liar and, therefore, could not point to his own classroom.

151. The old one was "expired." The new one is "changed." Both passwords contain the letters e and d.

152. Everything (each word) in West Hickory must contain double letters.

153. Izzy's stepdad used the hammer to install a shelf high up on the wall. He placed the video game console and the controllers up on the shelf out of Izzy's reach; however, Izzy's stepdad could still reach them.

154. The local business owner has a fish. See the table below:

Apartment	#1	#2	#3	#4	#5
Door Material	Cement	Glass	Brick	Metal	Wood
Job	Nurse	Graphic Designer	Teacher	Local Business Owner	Author
Favorite Drink	Water	Tea	Milk	Coffee	Orange Juice
Car	Convertible	Sedan	SUV	Motorcycle	Van
Pet	Cat	Iguana	Birds	Fish	Dog

THE ULTIMATE TALLY

Use the Ultimate Tally if you are working your way through the whole book before counting your score. Write the players' names in the left column and use the right column to tally your correct answers. You can use hash marks or write down the riddle numbers you answered correctly. (Tip: Tracking the riddle numbers will help you remember which riddles you've already mastered!) Add up each player's score. Whoever has won the most riddles will be crowned the Ultimate Riddle Champion!

PLAYER	SCORE
_____	
_____	
_____	
_____	

PLAYER

SCORE

Hi, parents and caregivers,

We hope your child enjoyed *The Ultimate Riddle Game for Kids*. If you have any questions or concerns about this book, or have received a damaged copy, please contact customerservice@penguinrandomhouse.com. We're here and happy to help.

Also, please consider writing a review on your favorite retailer's website to let others know what you and your child thought of the book!

Sincerely,
The Zeitgeist Team